OTHERWORLDS

Otherworlds

Poems of the Mysterious

Compiled by
Judith Nicholls

With illustrations by
Shirley Felts

faber and faber
LONDON · BOSTON

First published in 1995
by Faber and Faber Limited
3 Queen Square London WC1N 3AU

Photoset by Wilmaset Ltd, Birkenhead, Wirral
Printed in England by
Clays Ltd, St Ives Plc

This collection © Judith Nicholls, 1995
Illustrations © Shirley Felts, 1995

Judith Nicholls is hereby identified as the editor of this
work in accordance with Section 77 of the Copyright, Designs
and Patents Act 1988

A CIP record for this book
is available from the British Library

ISBN 0–571–17216–4

For Dominique and Neil H.,
with love

Contents

Silent is the house . . .

Only he who sees . . .

I saw a peacock . . .

[ix]

The night grows dark . . .

Introduction

'There are more things in heaven and earth, Horatio,
Than are dreamt of in your philosophy.'
William Shakespeare

Einstein once asserted, 'The most beautiful experience we can have is the mysterious.' 'The mysterious', in one form or another, is something poets have striven to express in words since poetry first began. When I was gathering work for this anthology one poet wrote to me that almost all of her poems, both for children and adults, seemed to have 'a whiff of another dimension'. Despite this long-standing fascination, 'the mysterious' is notably difficult to define.

I wanted to gather here just a selection of the kind of poems that might, together, go some way towards that definition. I was looking for poems which touch upon feelings or events which are unexplained or inexplicable in everyday or scientific terms; for poems which give experiences of some kind of reality beyond 'normal' understanding; poems which, often for reasons other than fear, create a shiver down the spine.

Sometimes this sense of the mysterious may be associated with a particular tale, such as that of the *Mary Celeste*; sometimes it relates closely to a sense of the miraculous. Blake's 'The Tyger' is a well-known example of a poem which creates in just a few words a kind of divine sense of wonder. Some poems *tell* of the mysterious, others *create* the mysterious in their own echoes and rhythms; in some the telling and the showing are happily inextricable. Philip Larkin's 'Legend' comes to mind, Walter de la Mare's 'The Song of the Mad

Prince' and Yeats's 'The Song of Wandering Aengus'. A similar, though highly individual, felicity of touch occurs time and again in the poems of Emily Dickinson. The impact of poems such as these is unfading. It's hardly surprising that many of them have been so much anthologized; it would be difficult to omit all of them in an anthology of the mysterious in spite of that.

'There is more to earth/than dream the mind', sings Grace Nichols in the final poem here. This anthology aims to give a glimpse of just some of those mysterious *Otherworlds*.

Judith Nicholls
September 1993

I saw eternity . . .

First Morning

I was there on that first morning of creation
when heaven and earth occupied one space
and no one had heard of the human race.

I was there on that first morning of creation
when a river rushed from the belly of an egg
and a mountain rose from a golden yolk.

I was there on that first morning of creation
when the waters parted like magic cloth
and the birds shook feathers at the first joke.

John Agard

Birth

There is no mystery on Earth
Exceeds the mighty miracle of birth.
Not all the fearful mystery of death
Surpasses that first breaking into light
And timid, fragile breath.

John Kitching

Firstborn

For years I dreamt you
my lost child, a face unpromised.
I gathered you in, gambling,
making maps over your head.
You were the beginning of a wish
and when I finally held you,
like some mother-cat I looked you over –
my dozy lone-traveller set down at last.

               So much for maps,
I tried to etch you in, little stranger
wrapped like a Japanese doll.

You opened your fish-eyes and stared,
slowly your bunched fists
bracing on air.

Katherine Gallagher

When I was a Child . . .
(*from* The Third Century)

The Corn was Orient and Immortal Wheat, which never
should be reaped, nor was ever sown. I thought it had
stood from everlasting to everlasting. The Dust and Stones
of the Street were as Precious as GOLD. The Gates were at
first the End of the World.

Thomas Traherne (1637–74)

Flowers and Moonlight on the Spring River

The evening river is level and motionless –
The spring colours just open to their full.
Suddenly a wave carries the moon away
And the tidal water comes with its freight of stars.

Yang-ti (Emperor of the Sui dynasty, 605–17)
(translated by Arthur Waley)

Davy by Starlight

Climbing rung after rung the scrambling-
   net of the skies,
Over roof-top and quayside crane
   went Davy's eyes.

They glinted in primitive wonder
   with starlight thrown
From suns that cooled a million years
   before he was born.

And rung after painful rung, his slow
   thoughts climbed the night –
Cat-walking roof and chimney-pot
   at a dizzying height –
Till they slipped and were tumbled headlong
   into strange seas of light!

Raymond Wilson

from Stray Birds

Let me think that there is one among those stars
that guides my life through the dark unknown.

Rabindranath Tagore (1861–1941)

from The World

I saw eternity the other night
Like a great ring of pure and endless light,
    All calm, as it was bright;
And, round beneath it, time, in hours, days, years,
    Driven by the spheres,
Like a vast shadow moved, in which the world
    And all her train were hurled.

Henry Vaughan (1622?–95)

from Stray Birds

'What language is thine, O sea?'
    'The language of eternal question.'
'What language is thy answer, O sky?'
    'The language of eternal silence.'

Rabindranath Tagore (1861–1941)

The Starlight Night

Look at the stars! look, look up at the skies!
  O look at all the fire-folk sitting in the air!
  The bright boroughs, the circle-citadels there!
Down in dim woods the diamond delves! the elves'-eyes!
The grey lawns cold where gold, where quickgold lies!
  Wind-beat whitebeam; airy abeles set on a flare!
  Flake-doves sent floating forth at a farmyard scare! –
Ah well! it is all a purchase, all is a prize.

Buy then! Bid then! – What? – Prayer, patience, alms, vows
Look, look! a May-mess, like on orchard boughs!
  Look! March-bloom, like on mealed-with-yellow sallow!
These are indeed the barn: within-doors house
The shocks. This piece-bright paling shuts the spouse
  Christ home, Christ and his mother and all his hallows.

Gerard Manley Hopkins (1844–89)

The Unending Sky

I could not sleep for thinking of the sky,
  The unending sky, with all its million suns
Which turn their planets everlastingly
  In nothing, where the fire-haired comet runs.
If I could sail that nothing, I should cross
  Silence and emptiness with dark stars passing;
Then, in the darkness, see a point of gloss
  Burn to a glow, and glare, and keep massing,
And rage into a sun with wandering planets,
  And drop behind; and then, as I proceed,
See his last light upon his last moon's granites
  Die to a dark that would be night indeed:
Night where my soul might sail a million years
In nothing, not even Death, not even tears.

  John Masefield (1878–1967)

Dreams

Here we are all, by day; by night we're hurled
By dreams, each one, into a several world.

  Robert Herrick (1591–1674)

Stillness

When the words rustle no more,
  And the last work's done,
When the bolt lies deep in the door,
  And Fire, our Sun,
Falls on the dark-laned meadows of the floor;

When from the clock's last chime to the next chime
  Silence beats his drum,
And Space with gaunt grey eyes and her brother Time
  Wheeling and whispering come,
She with the mould of form and he with the loom of rhyme:

Then twittering out in the night my thought-birds flee,
  I am emptied of all my dreams:
I only hear Earth turning, only see
  Ether's long bankless streams,
And only know I should drown if you laid not your hand on me.

James Elroy Flecker (1884–1915)

I stepped from Plank to Plank

I stepped from Plank to Plank
A slow and cautious way
The Stars about my Head I felt
About my Feet the Sea.

I knew not but the next
Would be my final inch –
This gave me that precarious Gait
Some call Experience.

Emily Dickinson (1830–86)

There is a spirit in the woods . . .

from David and Bethsabe

God, in the whizzing of a pleasant wind,
Shall march upon the tops of mulberry trees.

George Peele (1558?–97?)

from An Autumn Effect

The spirit of the place seemed to be all attention; the wood
listened as I went and held its breath to number my
footfalls.

Robert Louis Stevenson (1850–94)

from Wanderings in June

The whispering voice of woods and streams
That breathe of Eden still.

John Clare (1793–1864)

Midnight Forest

Who wanders wild
in moon and puffball light
where night sleeps black
and spiders creep?
What is that sound
that stills the air?
Whose is the breath
that rustles oak and fir?
Beware,
the tree-gods stir.

Judith Nicholls

from The Tempest

Be not afeard; the isle is full of noises,
Sounds and sweet airs, that give delight, and hurt not.
Sometimes a thousand twangling instruments
Will hum about mine ears; and sometimes voices,
That, if I then had waked after long sleep,
Will make me sleep again; and then, in dreaming,
The clouds methought would open, and show riches
Ready to drop upon me; that, when I waked,
I cried to dream again.

William Shakespeare (1564–1616)

There is a Charm in Solitude that cheers

There is a charm in Solitude that cheers
A feeling that the world knows nothing of
A green delight the wounded mind endears
After the hustling world is broken off
Whose whole delight was crime at good to scoff
Green solitude his prison pleasure yields
The bitch fox heeds him not – birds seem to laugh
He lives the Crusoe of his lonely fields
Which dark green oaks his noontide leisure shields

John Clare (1793–1864)

Whispers in the Wood

Did you not see me when you came into the wood?
Did you not? You didn't see me at all?
I wasn't hiding. I was watching for you.
Did you notice the colour of the dry stone wall
Shift from goose-grey to buttery? Didn't you at all?

You say it often does that. Yes. And I'm usually there.
But perhaps, instead, you heard me? Surely you heard?
Nothing? You heard nothing? The wood went suddenly
    silent?
That was me. The trill of an unknown bird
Through the copse? It could have been me you heard.

Did you notice a spider web that billowed like a sail?
Were you not visited by an unexpected thought
About someone who may have lived in this wood
At some time in the past? Were you caught
Unawares? Were you sad? . . . I was that thought.

I have been watching for you, and waiting.
You like this wood. So do I. I know you well.
You do not see me but I'm not far away.
When you come here to play, do you not catch a smell
Sometimes in autumn? Do you never sense my presence?
    Well . . . ?

Gerard Benson

The Way through the Woods

They shut the road through the woods
Seventy years ago.
Weather and rain have undone it again,
And now you would never know
There was once a road through the woods
Before they planted the trees.
It is underneath the coppice and heath,
And the thin anemones.
Only the keeper sees
That, where the ring-dove broods,
And the badgers roll at ease,
There was once a road through the woods.

Yet, if you enter the woods
Of a summer evening late,
When the night-air cools on the trout-ringed pools
Where the otter whistles his mate,
(They fear not men in the woods,
Because they see so few)
You will hear the beat of a horse's feet,
And the swish of a skirt in the dew,
Steadily cantering through
The misty solitudes,
As though they perfectly knew
The old lost road through the woods . . .
But there is no road through the woods.

Rudyard Kipling (1865–1936)

The Flint

Who lived in these ancient woods?
Many thousand years ago
small men made their dwellings here –
lugged the great stones to and fro
and beneath a sheltering bough
ate, and slept, as I do now.

Who last held this flint? I guess
someone sharpened it to be
a precious weapon . . . kept it safe . . .
used it often, skilfully,
carved an arrowhead, and slit
the creature's throat he slew with it.

Who felt spirits in the trees?
Saw the sun rise like a god
on its journey east to west?
Who sniffed water, understood
where it wandered through the ground
and marked the spot it might be found?

Who walked on this ancient track?
Short and muscular, he wore
skins to cover him, and lit
fires to warm the winter's core.
In my hand (how strange it is!)
I hold the flint he held in his.

Jean Kenward

from The Bacchae

Will they ever come to me, ever again,
  The long long dances
On through the dark till the dim stars wane?
  Shall I feel the dew on my throat, and the stream
  Of wind in my hair? Shall our white feet gleam
    In the dim expanses?
Oh, feet of a fawn to the greenwood fled,
  Alone in the grass and the loveliness;
Leap of the hunted, no more in dread,
  Beyond the snares and the deadly press:
Yet a voice and a fear and a haste of hounds;
  A wildly labouring, fiercely fleet,
Onward yet by river and glen.
  Is it joy or terror, ye storm-swift feet?
To the dear lone lands untroubled of men,
Where no voice sounds, and amid the shadowy green
The little things of the woodland live unseen.

  Euripides (c.484–07 BC)
  (translated by Gilbert Murray)

November Night

Listen . . .
With faint dry sound,
Like steps of passing ghosts,
The leaves, frost-crisped, break from the trees
And fall.

  Adelaide Crapsey (1878–1914)

Now! says Time

NOW! Says Time,
and lifts his finger,
and the leaf on the lime
may not linger.
When Time utters
NOW! and lifts
his finger, the oakleaf flutters
and drifts,
and elm and beech
let a leaf fall from the bough
when, finger lifted, to each
Time says NOW!

Eleanor Farjeon (1881–1965)

Trees cannot name the Seasons

Trees cannot name the seasons
Nor flowers tell the time.
But when the sun shines
And they are charged with light,
They take a day-long breath.
What we call 'night'
Is their soft exhalation.

And when joints creak yet again
And the dead skin of leaves falls,
Trees don't complain
Nor mourn the passing of hours.
What we call 'winter'
Is simply hibernation.

And as continuation
Comes to them as no surprise
They feel no need
To divide and itemize.
Nature has never needed reasons
For flowers to tell the time
Or trees put a name to seasons.

Roger McGough

from Proverbs of Hell

A fool sees not the same tree
that a wise man sees.

William Blake (1757–1827)

from Revelation

And he shewed me a pure river of water of life, clear as crystal, proceeding out of the throne of God and of the Lamb.

In the midst of the street of it, and on either side of the river, was there the tree of life, which bare twelve manner of fruits, and yielded her fruit every month: and the leaves of the tree were for the healing of the nations.

Authorized King James Version

When men and mountains meet . . .

from Gnomic Verses

Great things are done when men and mountains meet;
This is not done by jostling in the street.

   William Blake (1757–1827)

from King Lear

                    . . . So we'll live,
And pray, and sing, and tell old tales, and laugh
At gilded butterflies, and hear poor rogues
Talk of court news; and we'll talk with them too,
Who loses and who wins; who's in, who's out;
And take upon's the mystery of things . . .

   William Shakespeare (1564–1616)

How the old Mountains drip with Sunset

How the old Mountains drip with Sunset
How the Hemlocks burn –
How the Dun Brake is draped in Cinder
By the Wizard Sun –

How the old Steeples hand the Scarlet
Till the Ball is full –
Have I the lip of the Flamingo
That I dare to tell?

Then, how the Fire ebbs like Billows –
Touching all the Grass
With a departing – Sapphire – feature –
As a Duchess passed –

How a small Dusk crawls on the Village
Till the Houses blot
And the odd Flambeau, no men carry
Glimmer on the Street –

How it is Night – in Nest and Kennel –
And where was the Wood –
Just a Dome of Abyss is Bowing
Into Solitude –

These are the Visions flitted Guido –
Titian – never told –
Domenichino dropped his pencil –
Paralyzed, with Gold –

Emily Dickinson (1830–86)

Full Many a Glorious Morning have I seen
(*from* Sonnet 33)

Full many a glorious morning have I seen
Flatter the mountain tops with sovereign eye,
Kissing with golden face the meadows green,
Gilding pale streams with heavenly alchemy.

William Shakespeare (1564–1616)

from The Prelude, Book I

Lustily
I dipped my oars into the silent lake,
And, as I rose upon the stroke, my boat
Went heaving through the water like a swan;
When, from behind that craggy steep till then
The horizon's bound, a huge peak, black and huge,
As if with voluntary power instinct
Upreared its head. I struck and struck again,
And growing still in stature the grim shape
Towered up between me and the stars, and still,
For so it seemed, with purpose of its own
And measured motion like a living thing,
Strode after me. With trembling oars I turned,
And through the silent water stole my way
Back to the covert of the willow tree;
There in her mooring-place I left my bark, –
And through the meadows homeward went, in grave
And serious mood; but after I had seen
That spectacle, for many days, my brain
Worked with a dim and undetermined sense
Of unknown modes of being; o'er my thoughts
There hung a darkness, call it solitude
Or blank desertion. No familiar shapes
Remained, no pleasant images of trees,
Of sea or sky, no colours of green fields;
But huge and mighty forms, that do not live
Like living men, moved slowly through the mind
By day, and were a trouble to my dreams.

William Wordsworth (1770–1850)

The Merman

He was ploughing his single furrow
Through the green, heavy sward
Of water. I was sowing winter wheat
At the shoreline, when our farms met.

Not a furrow, quite, I argued.
Nothing would come of his long acre
But breaker growing out of breaker,
The wind-scythe, the rain-harrow.

Had he no wish to own such land
As he might plough round in a day?
What of friendship, love? Such qualities?

He remembered these same fields of corn or hay
When swathes ran high along the ground,
Hearing the cries of one in difficulties.

Paul Muldoon

from Isaiah

You will go out in joy and be led forth in peace; and the
mountains and the hills will burst into song before you, and
all the trees of the field will clap their hands.

Authorized King James Version

from Shadows in the Water

In unexperienc'd Infancy
Many a sweet Mistake doth ly:
Mistake tho false, intending tru;
A *Seeming* somewhat more than *View*;
   That doth instruct the Mind
   In Things that ly behind,
And many Secrets to us show
which afterwards we com to know.

Thus did I by the Water's brink
Another World beneath me think;
And while the lofty spacious Skies
Reversed there abus'd mine Eys,
   I fancy'd other Feet
   Came mine to touch and meet;
As by som Puddle I did play
Another World within it lay.

Beneath the Water Peeple drown'd.
Yet with another Hev'n crown'd,
In spacious Regions seem'd to go
Freely moving to and fro:
   In bright and open Space
   I saw their very face;
Eys, Hands, and Feet they had like mine;
Another Sun did with them shine.

'Twas strange that Peeple there should walk,
And yet I could not hear them talk:
That throu a little watry Chink,
Which one dry Ox or Horse might drink,
  We other Worlds should see,
  Yet not admitted be;
And other Confines there behold
Of Light and Darkness, Heat and Cold.

I call'd them oft, but call'd in vain;
No Speeches we could entertain:
Yet did I there expect to find
Som other World, to pleas my Mind.
  I plainly saw by these
  A new *Antipodes*,
Whom, tho they were so plainly seen,
A Film kept off that stood between.

. . .

Of all the Play-mates which I knew
That here I do the Image view
In other Selvs; what can it mean?
But that below the purling Stream
  Som unknown Joys there be
  Laid up in Store for me;
To which I shall, when that thin Skin
Is broken, be admitted in.

Thomas Traherne (1637–74)

Strange and lonely seas . . .

Echoes

The sea laments
The livelong day,
Fringing its waste of sand;
Cries back the wind from the whispering shore –
No words I understand:

Yet echoes in my heart a voice,
As far, as near, as these –
The wind that weeps,
The solemn surge
Of strange and lonely seas.

Walter de la Mare (1873–1956)

The Galley of Count Arnaldos

Ah! what pleasant visions haunt me
    As I gaze upon the sea!
All the old romantic legends,
    All my dreams, come back to me.

Sails of silk and ropes of sandal,
    Such as gleam in ancient lore;
And the singing of the sailors,
    And the answer from the shore!

Most of all, the Spanish ballad
    Haunts me oft, and tarries long,
Of the noble Count Arnaldos
    And the sailor's mystic song.

Telling how the Count Arnaldos,
    With his hawk upon his hand,
Saw a fair and stately galley,
    Steering onward to the land; –

How he heard the ancient helmsman
    Chant a song so wild and clear,
That the sailing sea-bird slowly
    Poised upon the mast to hear,

Till his soul was full of longing,
    And he cried, with impulse strong, –
'Helmsman! for the love of heaven,
    Teach me, too, that wondrous song!'

'Wouldst thou,' – so the helmsman answered, –
  'Learn the secret of the sea?
Only those who brave its dangers
  Comprehend its mystery!'

Henry Wadsworth Longfellow (1807–82)

Goodwin Sands

I have seen the pale gulls circle
against the restless sky;
I have heard the dark winds crying
as dusk-drawn clouds wheel by.

But the waiting waves still whisper
of shadowy ocean lands,
of twisting tides and of secrets
that lie beneath the Sands.

I have seen the wild weeds' tangle
and smelt the salted squall;
I have seen the moon rise from the seas,
and felt the long night's fall.

But whose are the voices that echo
from the shifting ocean lands,
that tell of secrets buried
beneath the drifting Sands?

For many sail the Goodwins
and some return to shore;
but others ride in the falling tide
and those are seen no more.

And voices rise from the waters
beneath a restless sky:
in the dying light of coming night
the long-lost sailors sigh;
from the watery lands of Goodwin Sands
I hear the sailors cry.

   Judith Nicholls

Seafarer

longe sceolde
hrēran mid hondum   *hrīmcealde sǣ*

(He must for a long time move with his hands the ice-cold sea)
from The Wanderer (Anglo-Saxon)

I'm the one in the lifeboat
After the ship went down:
O never pity me for
The salty voyage home.

I'm the one undrowned
(Though I have come
Sorrowing seas across –
And the rest gone).

Gerda Mayer

Ariel's Song
(*from* The Tempest)

Full fathom five thy father lies;
   Of his bones are coral made;
Those are pearls that were his eyes:
   Nothing of him that doth fade,
But doth suffer a sea-change
Into something rich and strange.
Sea-nymphs hourly ring his knell:
                Ding-dong
Hark! now I hear them, – Ding-dong, bell.

William Shakespeare (1564–1616)

The Sands of Dee

'Oh Mary, go and call the cattle home,
And call the cattle home,
And call the cattle home,
Across the sands of Dee!'
The western wind was wild and dank with foam,
And all alone went she.

The western tide crept up along the sand,
And o'er the sand,
And round and round the sand,
As far as eye could see.
The rolling mist came down and hit the land:
And never home came she.

'O is it weed, or fish, or floating hair –
A tress of golden hair,
A drowned maiden's hair,
Above the nets at sea?'
Was never salmon yet that shone so fair
Among the stakes of Dee.

They rowed her in across the rolling foam,
The cruel crawling foam,
The cruel hungry foam,
To her grave beside the sea;
But still the boatmen hear her call the cattle home,
Across the sands of Dee.

Charles Kingsley (1819–75)

Morwenstow

Where do you come from, sea,
To the sharp Cornish shore,
Leaping up to the raven's crag?
  From Labrador.

Do you grow tired, sea?
Are you weary ever
When the storms burst over your head?
  Never.

Are you hard as a diamond, sea,
As iron, as oak?
Are you stronger than flint or steel?
  And the lightning stroke.

Ten thousand years and more, sea,
You have gobbled your fill,
Swallowing stone and slate!
  I am hungry still.

When will you rest, sea?
  When moon and sun
  Ride only fields of salt water
  And the land is gone.

Charles Causley

from Dover Beach

The sea is calm to-night,
The tide is full, the moon lies fair
Upon the Straits; – on the French coast the light
Gleams and is gone; the cliffs of England stand,
Glimmering and vast, out in the tranquil bay.
Come to the window, sweet is the night air!
Only from the long line of spray
Where the ebb meets the moon-blanch'd sand,
Listen! you hear the grating roar
Of pebbles which the waves suck back, and fling,
At their return, up the high strand,
Begin, and cease, and then again begin,
With tremulous cadence slow, and bring
The eternal note of sadness in.

Matthew Arnold (1822–88)

from The Sea's Limits

Consider the sea's listless chime:
  Time's self it is, made audible,
  The murmur of the earth's own shell.
Secret continuance sublime
  Is the sea's end: our sight may pass
  No furlong further. Since time was,
This sound hath told the lapse of time.

No quiet, which is death's, – it hath
  The mournfulness of ancient life,
  Enduring always at dull strife.
As the world's heart of rest and wrath,
  Its painful pulse is in the sands.
  Last utterly, the whole sky stands,
Grey and not known, along its path . . .

Gather a shell from the strown beach
  And listen at its lips: they sigh
  The same desire and mystery,
The echo of the whole sea's speech.
  And all mankind is thus at heart
  Not anything but what thou art:
And Earth, Sea, Man, are all in each.

Dante Gabriel Rossetti (1828–82)

The Shell

And then I pressed the shell
  Close to my ear
And listened well,
And straightway like a bell
  Came low and clear
The slow, sad murmur of far distant seas,
Whipped by an icy breeze
  Upon a shore
Windswept and desolate.
  It was a sunless strand that never bore
The footprint of a man,
  Nor felt the weight
Since time began
Of any human quality or stir
Save what the dreary winds and waves incur.
And in the hush of waters was the sound
Of pebbles rolling round,
For ever rolling with a hollow sound.
And bubbling sea-weeds as the waters go
Swish to and fro
Their long, cold tentacles of slimy grey.
There was no day,
Nor ever came a night
Setting the stars alight
To wonder at the moon:
Was twilight only and the frightened croon,
Smitten to whimpers, of the dreary wind

And waves that journeyed blind –
And then I loosed my ear – oh, it was sweet
To hear a cart go jolting down the street!

James Stephens (1882–1950)

Silent is the house . . .

Trespassers Will . . .

The sign says PRIVATE.
Tall scrolled-iron gates
are rusted shut.
Nobody comes here,
but . . .
>   now and again
>   was that the dull chink
>   of a padlock chain?

Inside, the drive is lost
in old-man's-beard and brambles,
grass so long uncut
it might conceal a man-trap
but . . .
>   crisp, clear
>   as breaking glass, a child
>   laughs. Can't you hear?

The trees close round
like lawyers whispering the clauses
of a long-forgotten will.
They won't tell you a thing.
But still . . .
>   though no one spoke
>   you feel you've come too late
>   to join the joke.

Sometimes you glimpse
a gutted tower, empty windows.
Other times they fill
with odd long slants of sunset.
Still . . .

       did someone call?
       Was it a bird? Your name?
       You climb the wall.

Look. Nothing. Listen. Nothing.
Through scents of leaves and soil
here comes a sweet sharp whiff
of . . . what? You might remember
if . . .

       you find the wooden gate
       into the garden. And you wonder,
       am I late?

It's later than you can imagine.
Ease the latch. The wood is soft
with mildew though the hinge is stiff.
It crumbles in, into a sudden hush,
no *but* or *if*.

       It's what you had to do.
       This is a private party.
       They're expecting you.

Philip Gross

The New House

Now first, as I shut the door,
  I was alone
In the new house; and the wind
  Began to moan.

Old at once was the house,
  And I was old;
My ears were teased with the dread
  Of what was foretold,

Nights of storm, days of mist, without end;
  Sad days when the sun
Shone in vain: old griefs and griefs
  Not yet begun.

All was foretold me; naught
  Could I foresee;
But I learned how the wind would sound
  After these things should be.

Edward Thomas (1878–1917)

The Listeners

'Is there anybody there?' said the Traveller,
    Knocking on the moonlit door;
And his horse in the silence champed the grasses
    Of the forest's ferny floor:
And a bird flew up out of the turret,
    Above the Traveller's head:
And he smote upon the door a second time;
    'Is there anybody there?' he said.
But no one descended to the Traveller;
    No head from the leaf-fringed sill
Leaned over and looked into his grey eyes,
    Where he stood perplexed and still.
But only a host of phantom listeners
    That dwelt in the lone house then
Stood listening in the quiet of the moonlight
    To that voice from the world of men:
Stood thronging the faint moonbeams on the dark stair,
    That goes down to the empty hall,
Hearkening in an air stirred and shaken
    By the lonely Traveller's call.
And he felt in his heart their strangeness,
    Their stillness answering his cry,
While his horse moved, cropping the dark turf,
    'Neath the starred and leafy sky;
For he suddenly smote on the door, even
    Louder, and lifted his head:
'Tell them I came, and no one answered,
    That I kept my word,' he said.
Never the least stir made the listeners
    Though every word he spake
Fell echoing through the shadowiness of the still house

From the one man left awake:
Ay, they heard his foot upon the stirrup,
  And the sound of iron on stone,
And how the silence surged softly backward,
  When the plunging hoofs were gone.

  Walter de la Mare (1873–1956)

Only

Only a tap drip, dripping
In the courtyard, by the wall
Where cushiony mosses flourish
And fleshy ferns grow tall.
Only a shutter rattling
When the wind decides to call,
Only a creeping of shadows
As night begins to fall.
Only a whisper of memories
In the lonely air of the hall.

  John Cotton

Vulnerable

Everything is vulnerable at sunrise.
Houses are blurred at the edge by the creeping light.
They are not yet upright, not yet property.

Inside the houses
Bodies and beds are still to be disentangled,
Naked, bearded, sheeted, flowing, breathing,
With no cosmetic except the morning's colouring.

No body has had time to put on its uniform
To arm itself with the safe and usual phrases,
To start counting, considering, feeling hungry,
Being man or woman . . .

They lie scattered, invisible, soft, lovable,
Under the surreptitious hands of the sunrise,
The touching light.

They are not yet upright, not yet property.

Elma Mitchell

The Strange House

(Max Gate, AD 2000)

'I hear the piano playing –
    Just as a ghost might play.'
' – O, but what are you saying?
    There's no piano today;
Their old one was sold and broken:
    Years past it went amiss.'
' – I heard it, or shouldn't have spoken:
    A strange house, this!

'I catch some undertone here,
    From some one out of sight.'
' – Impossible; we are alone here,
    And shall be through the night.'
' – The parlour-door – what stirred it?'
    ' – No one: no soul's in range.'
' – But, anyhow, I heard it,
    And it seems strange!

'Seek my own room I cannot –
    A figure is on the stair!'
' – What figure? Nay, I scan not
    Any one lingering there.
A bough outside is waving,
    And that's its shade by the moon.'
' – Well, all is strange! I am craving
    Strength to leave soon.'

' – Ah, maybe you've some vision
    Of showings beyond our sphere;
Some sight, sense, intuition
    Of what once happened here?
The house is old; they've hinted
    It once held two love-thralls,
And they may have imprinted
        Their dreams on its walls?

'They were – I think 'twas told me –
    Queer in their works and ways;
The teller would often hold me
    With weird tales of those days.
Some folk can not abide here,
    But we – we do not care
Who loved, laughed, wept, or died here,
        Knew joy, or despair.'

Thomas Hardy (1840–1928)

Silent is the House

Silent is the house: all are laid asleep:
One, alone, looks out o'er the snow wreaths deep,
Watching every cloud, dreading every breeze
That whirls the 'wildering drift and bends the groaning trees.

Cheerful is the hearth, soft the matted floor;
Not one shivering gust creeps through pane or door;
The little lamp burns straight, its rays shoot strong and far;
I trim it well to be the wanderer's guiding-star.

Frown, my haughty sire; chide, my angry dame;
Set your slaves to spy, threaten me with shame!
But neither sire nor dame, nor prying serf shall know,
What angel nightly tracks that waste of frozen snow.

What I love shall come like visitant of air,
Safe in secret power from lurking human snare;
What loves me, no word of mine shall e'er betray,
Though for faith unstained my life must forfeit pay.

Burn, then, little lamp; glimmer straight and clear –
Hush! a rustling wing stirs, methinks, the air:
He for whom I wait, thus ever comes to me;
Strange Power! I trust thy might; trust thou my constancy.

Emily Brontë (1818–48)

One need not be a Chamber – to be Haunted –

One need not be a Chamber – to be Haunted –
One need not be a House –
The Brain has Corridors – surpassing
Material Place –

Far safer, of a Midnight Meeting
External Ghost
Than its interior Confronting –
That Cooler Host.

Far safer, through an Abbey gallop,
The Stones a'chase –
Than Unarmed, one's a'self encounter –
In lonesome Place –

Ourself behind ourself, concealed –
Should startle most –
Assassin hid in our Apartment
Be Horror's least.

The Body – borrows a Revolver –
He bolts the Door –
O'erlooking a superior spectre –
Or More –

Emily Dickinson (1830–86)

Only he who sees . . .

from Aurora Leigh

Earth's crammed with heaven,
And every common bush afire with God;
But only he who sees, takes off his shoes,
The rest sit round it and pluck blackberries . . .

Elizabeth Barrett Browning (1806–61)

The Diviner

Cut from the green hedge a forked hazel stick
That he held tight by the arms of the V:
Circling the terrain, hunting the pluck
Of water, nervous, but professionally

Unfussed. The pluck came sharp as a sting.
The rod jerked down with precise convulsions,
Spring water suddenly broadcasting
Through a green aerial its secret stations.

The bystanders would ask to have a try.
He handed them the rod without a word.
It lay dead in their grasp till nonchalantly
He gripped expectant wrists. The hazel stirred.

Seamus Heaney

The Song of Wandering Aengus

I went out to the hazel wood,
Because a fire was in my head,
And cut and peeled a hazel wand,
And hooked a berry to a thread;
And when white moths were on the wing,
And moth-like stars were flickering out,
I dropped the berry in a stream
And caught a little silver trout.

When I had laid it on the floor
I went to blow the fire aflame,
But something rustled on the floor,
And some one called me by my name:
It had become a glimmering girl
With apple blossom in her hair
Who called me by my name and ran
And faded through the brightening air.

Though I am old with wandering
Through hollow lands and hilly lands,
I will find out where she has gone,
And kiss her lips and take her hands;
And walk among long dappled grass,
And pluck till time and times are done
The silver apples of the moon,
The golden apples of the sun.

W. B. Yeats (1865–1939)

Rainforest

The forest drips and glows with green.
The tree-frog croaks his far-off song.
His voice is stillness, moss and rain
drunk from the forest ages long.

We cannot understand that call
unless we move into his dream,
where all is one and one is all
and frog and python are the same.

We with our quick dividing eyes
measure, distinguish and are gone.
The forest burns, the tree-frog dies,
yet one is all and all are one.

Judith Wright (1914–1982)

The Tyger

Tyger! Tyger! burning bright
In the forests of the night,
What immortal hand or eye
Could frame thy fearful symmetry?

In what distant deeps or skies
Burnt the fire of thine eyes?
On what wings dare he aspire?
What the hand dare sieze the fire?

And what shoulder, & what art,
Could twist the sinews of thy heart?
And when thy heart began to beat,
What dread hand? & what dread feet?

What the hammer? what the chain?
In what furnace was thy brain?
What the anvil? what dread grasp
Dare its deadly terrors clasp?

When the stars threw down their spears,
And water'd heaven with their tears,
Did he smile his work to see?
Did he who made the Lamb make thee?

Tyger! Tyger! burning bright
In the forests of the night,
What immortal hand or eye
Dare frame thy fearful symmetry?

William Blake (1757–1827)

The Burning Bush

When Moses, musing in the desert, found
The thorn bush spiking up from the hot ground,
And saw the branches, on a sudden, bear
The crackling yellow barberries of fire,

He searched his learning and imagination
For any logical, neat explanation,
And turned to go, but turned again and stayed,
And faced the fire and knew it for his God.

I too have seen the briar alight like coal,
The love that burns, the flesh that's ever whole,
And many times have turned and left it there,
Saying: 'It's prophecy – but metaphor.'

But stinging tongues like John the Baptist shout:
'That this is metaphor is no way out.
It's dogma too, or you make God a liar;
The bush is still a bush, and fire is fire.'

Norman Nicholson (1914–1982)

Humming Bird

I can imagine, in some otherworld
Primeval-dumb, far back
In that most awful stillness, that only gasped and hummed,
Humming-birds raced down the avenues.

Before anything had a soul,
While life was a heave of Matter, half inanimate,
This little bit chipped off in brilliance
And went whizzing through the slow, vast, succulent stems.

I believe there were no flowers then,
In the world where the humming-bird flashed ahead of
      creation.
I believe he pierced the slow vegetable veins with his long
       beak.

Probably he was big
As mosses, and little lizards, they say, were once big.
Probably he was a jabbing, terrifying monster.

We look at him through the wrong end of the long telescope
      of Time,
Luckily for us.

D. H. Lawrence (1885–1930)

Haiku

Far-off mountain peaks
Reflected in its eyes:
The dragonfly.

Kobayashi Issa (1763–1827)
(translated by Geoffrey Bownas and Anthony Thwaite)

Japanese Poet

Who are you?
I am the bird
that sits in the tree
singing.
I am the bird.
I am the tree.

I am
the cherry blossom.
Sure, I am he
watching –
and watched. Ask not
who I may be.

Jean Kenward

from What is the Truth?

There's comfort in the Cow, my dear, she's mother to us all.
When Adam was a helpless babe, no mother heard him call.
The Moon saw him forsaken and she let a white star fall.

Beasts sharpened their noses when his cry came on the air.
Did a she-wolf nurse him with the wolf-cubs in her lair?
Or cuffed among rough bear-cubs was he suckled by a bear?

No, the gentle Cow came, with her queenly, stately tread,
Swinging her dripping udder, and she licked his face and
    head,
And ever since that moment on the Cow's love he has fed.

A man is but a bare baboon, with starlit frightened eyes.
As earth rolls into night he cheers himself with monkey
    cries
And wraps his head in dreams, but his lonely spirit flies

To sleep among the cattle in the warm breath of the herd.
Among the giant mothers, he lies without a word.
In timeless peace they chew their cuds, till the first bird

Lifts the earth back into the clock, the spirit back into the
    man.
But the herd stays in Paradise, where everything began,
Where the rivers are rivers of foaming milk and the eyes are
    African.

Ted Hughes

The Oxen

Christmas Eve, and twelve of the clock.
   'Now they are all on their knees,'
An elder said as we sat in a flock
   By the embers in hearthside ease.

We pictured the meek mild creatures where
   They dwelt in their strawy pen,
Nor did it occur to one of us there
   To doubt they were kneeling then.

So fair a fancy few would weave
   In these years! Yet, I feel,
If someone said on Christmas Eve,
   'Come; see the oxen kneel

'In the lonely barton by yonder coomb
   Our childhood used to know,'
I should go with him in the gloom,
   Hoping it might be so.

Thomas Hardy (1840–1928)

I saw a peacock . . .

I Saw a Peacock . . .

I saw a peacock with a fiery tail
I saw a blazing comet drop down hail
I saw a cloud wrapped with ivy round
I saw an oak creep on along the ground
I saw a pismire swallow up a whale
I saw the sea brim full of ale
I saw a Venice glass five fathom deep
I saw a well full of men's tears that weep
I saw red eyes all of a flaming fire
I saw a house bigger than the moon and higher
I saw the sun at twelve o'clock at night
I saw the Man that saw this wondrous sight.

Anon.

There was no Telling

There was no telling what it was.
Some thought it large, some thought it small,
Some called it round, though some said square –
Some swore it had no shape at all!

The same with temperature and colour.
This one said hot, that one said cold;
One called it purple, but another
Green – and a third said gold.

Its smell, they variously claimed,
Was sweet as woodbine, sour as sweat;
Its taste pure peppermint or parsnip
Or cyanide or vinaigrette.

They disagreed about its weight,
Its height, depth, length, until their jaws
Ached contradicting one another.
There was no telling what it was.

The truth is, each one took his rod,
Swearing the rest were deaf, dumb, blind,
And sloped off to a place apart:
Each fished the pool of his own dark mind.

Raymond Wilson

Stone Circles

The ones
who set these stones
were shrewd, star-wise.

They knew the skies.

And plotted points
where sun and moon
would sink and rise.

They knew to measure,
calculate and place.

Transported massive weight
through tracts of space.

But why they hauled these stones
and set them so,
we only guess,
we cannot surely know.

Their thoughts, their reasons,
their intense belief
have blown away
on vanished winds,
light as a leaf.

The meaning's lost.
The flesh is gone.
All we have now are stones,
standing abandoned here
like remnant bones.

Tony Mitton

from A Booke of Merrie Riddles, 1631

A ship there drives upon the tide,
that sailes doth beare, she hath no mast.
But one oare she hath on each side;
her sailes the snow in whitenesse passe.
In her front weares two lanthorns bright;
but when she is upon point to fall,
then lend an eare, for great delight
of musicke she affords to all.

Anon.

Riddle (*from* The Exeter Book)

My dress is silent when I tread the ground
Or stay at home or stir upon the waters.
Sometimes my trappings and the lofty air
Raise me above the dwelling-place of men,
And then the power of clouds carries me far
Above the people; and my ornaments
Loudly resound, send forth a melody
And clearly sing, when I am not in touch
With earth or water, but a flying spirit.

Anon. (10th century)

You're

Clownlike, happiest on your hands,
Feet to the stars, and moon-skulled,
Gilled like a fish. A common-sense
Thumbs-down on the dodo's mode.
Wrapped up in yourself like a spool,
Trawling your dark as owls do.
Mute as a turnip from the Fourth
Of July to All Fools' Day,
O high-riser, my little loaf.

Vague as fog and looked for like mail.
Farther off than Australia.
Bent-backed Atlas, our traveled prawn.
Snug as a bud and at home
Like a sprat in a pickle jug.
A creel of eels, all ripples.
Jumpy as a Mexican bean.
Right, like a well-done sum.
A clean slate, with your own face on.

Sylvia Plath (1932–63)

I will give my Love an Apple

I will give my love an apple without e'er a core,
I will give my love a house without e'er a door,
I will give my love a palace wherein she may be,
And she may unlock it without any key.

My head is the apple without e'er a core,
My mind is the house without e'er a door,
My heart is the palace wherein she may be,
And she may unlock it without any key.

Anon.

from The Girl's Own Book, 1844

(Compiled by Mrs Child)

I was, but am not; ne'er shall be again;
Myriads possess'd me, and possess'd in vain;
To some I proved a friend, to some a foe;
Some I exalted, others I laid low;
To some I gave the bliss that knows no sigh,
And some condemn'd to equal misery.
If conscious that we met, and but to sever,
Now say to whom you bade farewell for ever.

Anon.

The Song of the Mad Prince

Who said 'Peacock Pie'?
  The old King to the sparrow:
Who said, 'Crops are ripe'?
  Rust to the harrow:
Who said, 'Where sleeps she now?
  Where rests she now her head,
Bathed in eve's loveliness'?
  That's what I said.

Who said, 'Ay, mum's the word'?
  Sexton to willow:
Who said, 'Green dusk for dreams,
  Moss for a pillow'?
Who said, 'All Time's delight
  Hath she for narrow bed;
Life's troubled bubble broken'?
  That's what I said.

  Walter de la Mare (1873–1956)

The Mystery

I am the wind which breathes upon the sea,
I am the wave of the ocean,
I am the murmur of the billows,
I am the ox of the seven combats,
I am the vulture upon the rocks,
I am a beam of the sun,
I am the fairest of plants,
I am a wild boar in valour,
I am a salmon in the water,
I am a lake in the plain,
I am a word of science,
I am the point of the lance in battle,
I am the God who creates in the head the fire.
Who is it who throws light into the meeting on the mountain?
Who announces the ages of the moon?
Who teaches the place where couches the sun?

Anon.

I'll tell you a tale . . .

Lock up Your Clocks

The grandfather clock in the hall
like a perfect butler stands aside
by day. If it speaks, it's only,
tactfully, to fill a silence.
   Until night-time . . .

Then bury your head if you will
in your pillow. You can't help but hear
that weighty footfall through
deserted rooms downstairs. Clocks
   bide their time.

The video recorder flickers green
beneath the TV table. It's alert
as a spider, busy netting dreams
from the airwaves while we're sleeping.
   Lights-out time

and everywhere and nowhere rise
small clockwork cries, squeaky-creaky
like rain-forest frogs or, digital,
the brittle whirr of insect wings.
   Bad time

to be awake. The ticker in your chest
picks up the threat. The night's alive
with tapped-out messages on frequencies
we can't quite catch, or won't, or not
   in time –

like yellow teeth, like claws at work
on the bars of the cage . . . A scratching
at the cell wall . . . Stropping of long knives,
short whispers: *Brothers, soon will come*
  the time . . .

The stroke of one. The town-hall clock.
Far off, another answers, slightly
  out of time.

Philip Gross

Only One God?

The Misses Lafferty live at 88.
Frail as fishbones, they walk
like whispers, always on tip-toe,
trailing peacock tails of scarves,
half-finished sentences and
the scent of dusty lavender.

They smile their bruised-petal smiles,
finger rosaries, ignore blood spilling
from pictures of dying saints.
We hear them call to each other
in high sweet voices, old-fashioned
shoes ticking across the lino.

They are left-overs from another
generation, still to come to grips
with Hoovers and television sets.
Bookcases bend beneath the weight
of encyclopaedias, volumes of Dickens,
the lesser poets, Shakespeare.

'Pop next door,' says our mother
when we're stumped by topic work.
'Ask the ladies.' We knock, wait.
Bolts are unbolted, locks unlocked.
We step into the hall, mirror-image
of our own, unlit, unfamiliar.

The Misses Lafferty smell purple,
like their mysterious religion.
They loan us books, mark pages,
breathe explanations. We gasp
our thanks, rush back to home ground,
the very devil at our heels.

Moira Andrew

Unwelcome

We were young, we were merry, we were very very wise,
   And the door stood open at our feast,
When there passed us a woman with the West in her eyes,
   And a man with his back to the East.

O, still grew the hearts that were beating so fast,
   The loudest voice was still.
The jest died away on our lips as they passed,
   And the rays of July struck chill.

The cups of red wine turn'd pale on the board,
   The white bread black as soot.
The hound forgot the hand of her lord,
   She fell down at his foot.

Low let me lie, where the dead dog lies,
   Ere I sit me down again at a feast,
When there passes a woman with the West in her eyes,
   And a man with his back to the East.

Mary Coleridge (1861–1907)

The Wife of Usher's Well

There lived a wife at Usher's Well,
    And a wealthy wife was she;
She had three stout and stalwart sons,
    And sent them o'er the sea.

They hadna been a week from her,
    A week but barely ane,
Whan word came to the carline wife
    That her three sons were gane.

They hadna been a week from her,
    A week but barely three,
Whan word came to the carlin wife
    That her sons she'd never see.

'I wish the wind may never cease,
    Nor fashes in the flood,
Till my three sons come hame to me,
    In earthly flesh and blood.'

It fell about the Martinmass,
    When nights are lang and mirk,
The carlin wife's three sons came hame,
    And their hats were o' the birk.

It neither grew in syke nor ditch,
    Nor yet in ony sheugh;
But at the gates o' Paradise,
    That birk grew fair eneugh.

'Blow up the fire, my maidens,
    Bring water from the well;
For a' my house shall feast this night,
    Since my three sons are well.'

And she has made to them a bed,
  She's made it large and wide,
And she's ta'en her mantle her about,
  Sat down at the bed-side.

. . .

Up then crew the red, red cock,
  And up and crew the gray;
The eldest to the youngest said,
  ' 'Tis time we were away.'

The cock he hadna craw'd but once,
  And clapp'd his wings at a',
When the youngest to the eldest said,
  'Brother, we must awa.

'The cock doth craw, the day doth daw,
  The channerin worm doth chide;
Gin we be mist out o' our place,
  A sair pain we maun bide.

'Fare ye weel, my mother dear!
  Fareweel to barn and byre!
And fare ye weel, the bonny lass
That kindles my mother's fire!'

  Anon.

from The Rime of the Ancient Mariner

Till noon we quietly sailed on,
Yet never a breeze did breathe:
Slowly and smoothly went the ship,
Moved onward from beneath.

Under the keel nine fathom deep,
From the land of mist and snow,
The spirit slid: and it was he
That made the ship to go.
The sails at noon left off their tune,
And the ship stood still also.

The Sun, right up above the mast,
Had fixed her to the ocean:
But in a minute she 'gan stir,
With a short uneasy motion –
Backwards and forwards half her length
With a short uneasy motion.

Then like a pawing horse let go,
She made a sudden bound:
It flung the blood into my head,
And I fell down in a swound.

How long in that same fit I lay,
I have not to declare;
But ere my living life returned,
I heard and in my soul discerned
Two voices in the air.

'Is it he?' quoth one, 'Is this the man?
By him who died on cross,
With his cruel bow he laid full low
The harmless Albatross.

'The spirit who bideth by himself
In the land of mist and snow,
He loved the bird that loved the man
Who shot him with his bow.'

The other was a softer voice,
As soft as honey-dew:
Quoth he, 'The man hath penance done,
And penance more will do.'

Samuel Taylor Coleridge (1772–1834)

Mary Celeste

Only the wind sings
in the riggings,
the hull creaks a lullaby;
a sail lifts gently
like a message
pinned to a vacant sky.
The wheel turns
over bare decks,
shirts flap on a line;
only the song of the lapping waves
beats steady time . . .

First mate,
off-duty from
the long dawn watch, begins
a letter to his wife, daydreams
of home.

The Captain's wife is late;
the child did not sleep
and breakfast has passed . . .
She, too, is missing home;
sits down at last to eat,
but can't quite force
the porridge down.
She swallows hard,
slices the top from her egg.

The second mate
is happy.
A four-hour sleep,
full stomach
and a quiet sea
are all he craves.
He has all three.

Shirts washed and hung, beds
made below, decks done, the boy
stitches a torn sail.

The Captain
has a good ear for a tune;
played his child to sleep
on the ship's organ.
Now, music left,
he checks his compass,
lightly tips the wheel,
hopes for a westerly.
Clear sky, a friendly sea,
fair winds for Italy.

The child now sleeps, at last,
head firmly pressed into her pillow
in a deep sea-dream.

*Then why are the gulls wheeling
like vultures in the sky?
Why was the child snatched
from her sleep? What drew
the Captain's cry?*

Only the wind replies
in the rigging,
and the hull creaks and sighs;
a sail spells out its message
over silent skies.
The wheel still turns
over bare decks,
shirts blow on the line;
the siren-song of lapping waves
still echoes over time.

Judith Nicholls

The North Ship

I saw three ships go sailing by,
Over the sea, the lifting sea,
And the wind rose in the morning sky,
And one was rigged for a long journey.

The first ship turned towards the west,
Over the sea, the running sea,
And by the wind was all possessed
And carried to a rich country.

The second turned towards the east,
Over the sea, the quaking sea,
And the wind hunted it like a beast
To anchor in captivity.

The third ship drove towards the north,
Over the sea, the darkening sea,
But no breath of wind came forth,
And the decks shone frostily.

The northern sky rose high and black
Over the proud unfruitful sea,
East and west the ships came back
Happily or unhappily:

But the third went wide and far
Into an unforgiving sea
Under a fire-spilling star,
And it was rigged for a long journey.

Philip Larkin (1922–85)

La Belle Dame Sans Merci

O, what can ail thee, knight at arms,
  Alone and palely loitering;
The sedge has withered from the lake,
  And no birds sing.

O, what can ail thee, knight at arms,
  So haggard and so woe-begone?
The squirrel's granary is full,
  And the harvest's done.

I see a lily on thy brow
  With anguish moist and fever-dew,
And on thy cheeks a fading rose
  Fast withereth too.

I met a lady in the meads,
  Full beautiful – a faery's child,
Her hair was long, her foot was light,
  And her eyes were wild.

I made a garland for her head,
  And bracelets too, and fragrant zone,
She looked at me as she did love,
  And made sweet moan.

I set her on my pacing steed
  And nothing else saw all day long;
For sideways would she lean, and sing
  A faery's song.

She found me roots of relish sweet,
  And honey wild and manna dew;
And sure in language strange she said –
  I love thee true.

She took me to her elfin grot,
  And there she wept and sighed full sore:
And there I shut her wild, wild eyes
  With kisses four.

And there she lullèd me asleep,
  And there I dreamed – Ah! Woe betide!
The latest dream I ever dreamed
  On the cold hill side.

I saw pale kings and princes too,
  Pale warriors, death-pale were they all:
They cried – 'La Belle Dame sans Merci
  Hath thee in thrall!'

I saw their starved lips in the gloam
  With horrid warning gapèd wide,
And I awoke, and found me here
  On the cold hill's side.

And this is why I sojourn here
  Alone and palely loitering,
Though the sedge is withered from the lake,
  And no birds sing.

  John Keats (1795–1821)

The Myrtle Bush grew Shady

'The myrtle bush grew shady
  Down by the ford.' –
'Is it even so?' said my lady.
  'Even so!' said my lord.
'The leaves are set too thick together
  For the point of a sword.'

'The arras in your room hangs close,
  No light between!
You wedded one of those
  That see unseen.' –
'Is it even so?' said the King's Majesty.
  'Even so!' said the Queen.

Mary Coleridge (1861–1907)

Hauntings

In the residue of lives to be read in the plans
Of staircases, fireplaces, doorways and wallpapers
Sketched on the walls of half-demolished dwellings.
In the echoes of past performances
That haunt the caverns of dark theatres.
In the faint rumblings of long-left classes
That disturb the hush of old deserted schools.
In the whispers of telephone conversations
That never quite connected
And drift on in the network of wires
That criss-cross the nation.
In the unwritten letters
Afloat in bottles on the oceans of the mind.
In the secret sharer,
An ideal you who lives inside your head.
In the hint of footsteps and hoof-clops
On ancient empty roads
Or pathless wastes.

John Cotton

The light of setting suns . . .

from Tintern Abbey

                I have felt
A presence that disturbs me with the joy
Of elevated thoughts; a sense sublime
Of something far more deeply interfused,
Whose dwelling is the light of setting suns,
And the round ocean and the living air,
And the blue sky, and in the mind of man:
A motion and a spirit, that impels
All thinking things, all objects of all thought,
And rolls through all things.

  William Wordsworth (1770–1850)

Who?

Who is that child I see wandering, wandering
Down by the side of the quivering stream?
Why does he seem not to hear, though I call to him?
Where does he come from, and what is his name?

Why do I see him at sunrise and sunset
Taking, in old-fashioned clothes, the same track?
Why, when he walks, does he cast not a shadow
Though the sun rises and falls at his back?

Why does the dust lie so thick on the hedgerow
By the great field where a horse pulls the plough?
Why do I see only meadows, where houses
Stand in a line by the riverside now?

Why does he move like a wraith by the water,
Soft as the thistledown on the breeze blown?
When I draw near him so that I may hear him,
Why does he say that his name is my own?

Charles Causley

To see a Ghost

To see a ghost
is to wait in a train
as another pulls in
the opposite way

and through the glass
only inches from yours
a face you almost
know from years

and years ago
stares back. Those eyes
meet yours. You blink
at each other's surprise

and see the *Oh!*
on each other's lips
as one train shudders
and begins to slip

away so smoothly
that neither can tell
which is moving,
which is still,

and who's going up,
who down, the line
and who's running on,
who out, of time.

Philip Gross

Heredity

I am the family face;
Flesh perishes, I live on,
Projecting trait and trace
Through time to times anon,
And leaping from place to place
Over oblivion.

The years-heired feature that can
In curve and voice and eye
Despise the human span
Of durance – that is I;
The eternal thing in man,
That heeds no call to die.

Thomas Hardy (1840–1928)

Guest

Is the kitchen tap still dripping?
You should always chain the door at nights.
Soon the roof will need repairing.
What's happening these days at the office?
Too much coffee agitates the nerves.
Now don't forget to spray the roses.
Do see the doctor about those twinges.

But tell me where you are! How is it there?
Are you in pain or bliss? And what is bliss?
Are you lonely? Do we live for ever?
How do you pass the time, if time there is?
Does God exist? Is God loving?
Why must his ways be so mysterious?
Is there a purpose in our living?

Why won't you speak of things that matter?
You used to be so wise, so serious.
Now all our talk is roofs and roses
Like neighbours chatting at the corner.

Here wisdom is as common as the air,
Great matters are the ground I tread.
Tell me, what weather are you having?
Are the planes still noisy overhead?
Ask my old mates how work is going –

Don't be angry, dear. This hasn't changed:
Those things we lack are what we covet.
I am the guest, the one to be indulged.

   D. J. Enright

Drummer Hodge

They throw in Drummer Hodge, to rest
   Uncoffined – just as found:
His landmark is a kopje-crest
   That breaks the veldt around;
And foreign constellations west
   Each night above his mound.

Young Hodge the Drummer never knew –
   Fresh from his Wessex home –
The meaning of the broad Karoo,
   The Bush, the dusty loam,
And why uprose to nightly view
   Strange stars amid the gloam.

Yet portion of that unknown plain
   Will Hodge for ever be;
His homely Northern breast and brain
   Grow to some Southern tree,
And strange-eyed constellations reign
   His stars eternally.

Thomas Hardy (1840–1928)

A Refusal to Mourn the Death, by
Fire, of a Child in London

Never until the mankind making
Bird beast and flower
Fathering and all humbling darkness
Tells with silence the last light breaking
And the still hour
Is come of the sea tumbling in harness

And I must enter again the round
Zion of the water bead
And the synagogue of the ear of corn
Shall I let pray the shadow of a sound
Or sow my salt seed
In the least valley of sackcloth to mourn

The majesty and burning of the child's death.
I shall not murder
The mankind of her going with a grave truth
Nor blaspheme down the stations of the breath
With any further
Elegy of innocence and youth.

Deep with the first dead lies London's daughter,
Robed in the long friends,
The grains beyond age, the dark veins of her mother,
Secret by the unmourning water
Of the riding Thames.
After the first death, there is no other.

Dylan Thomas (1914–53)

A Slumber did my Spirit seal

A slumber did my spirit seal;
  I had no human fears:
She seemed a thing that could not feel
  The touch of earthly years.

No motion has she now, no force;
  She neither hears nor sees;
Rolled round in earth's diurnal course,
  With rocks, and stones, and trees.

William Wordsworth (1770–1850)

The night grows dark . . .

from Darkness

I had a dream, which was not all a dream.
The bright sun was extinguished, and the stars
Did wander darkling in the eternal space,
Rayless, and pathless, and the icy earth
Swung blind and blackening in the moonless air;
Morn came and went – and came, and brought no day.

George Gordon, Lord Byron (1788–1824)

from Macbeth

I must become a borrower of the night . . .

William Shakespeare (1564–1616)

from The Gardener

The night grows dark and the road lonely. Fireflies gleam
among the leaves.

Who are you that follow me with stealthy silent steps?

Rabindranath Tagore (1861–1941)

The Midnight Skaters

The hop-poles stand in cones,
    The icy pond lurks under,
The pole-tops steeple to the thrones
    Of stars, sound gulfs of wonder;
But not the tallest there, 'tis said,
Could fathom to this pond's black bed.

Then is not death at watch
    Within those secret waters?
What wants he but to catch
    Earth's heedless sons and daughters?
With but a crystal parapet
Between, he has his engines set.

Then on, blood shouts, on, on,
    Twirl, wheel and whip above him,
Dance on this ball-floor thin and wan,
    Use him as though you love him;
Court him, elude him, reel and pass,
And let him hate you through the glass.

Edmund Blunden (1896–1974)

The Crickets sang

The Crickets sang
And set the Sun
And Workmen finished one by one
Their Seam the Day upon.

The low Grass loaded with the Dew
The Twilight stood, as Strangers do
With Hat in Hand, polite and new
To stay as if, or go.

A Vastness, as a Neighbor, came,
A Wisdom, without Face, or Name,
A Peace, as Hemispheres at Home
And so the Night became.

Emily Dickinson (1830–86)

Evening

It is the silent hour when they who roam,
   Seek shelter, on the earth, or ocean's breast;
It is the hour when travel finds a home,
   On deserts, or within the cot to rest.
   It is the hour when joy and grief are blest,
And Nature finds repose where'er she roves;
   It is the hour that lovers like the best,
When in the twilight shades, or darker groves,
The maiden wanders with the swain she loves.

The balmy hour when fond hearts fondly meet;
   The hour when dew like welcome rest descends
On wild-flowers, shedding forth their odours sweet;
   The hour when sleep lays foes as quiet friends; –
The hour when labour's toilworn journey ends,
And seeks the cot for sweet repose till morn; –
   The hour when prayer from all to God ascends; –
At twilight's hour love's softest sighs are born,
When lovers linger neath the flowering thorn.

Oh! at this hour I love to be abroad,
   Gazing upon the moonlit scene around
'Looking through Nature up to Nature's God'
   Regarding all with reverence profound!
   The wild flowers studding every inch of ground,
And trees, with dews bespangled, looking bright
   As burnished silver; – while the entrancing sound
Of melody, from the sweet bird of night,
Fills my whole soul with rapture and delight.

John Clare (1793–1864)

Out in the Dark

Out in the dark over the snow
The fallow fawns invisible go
With the fallow doe;
And the winds blow
Fast as the stars are slow.

Stealthily the dark haunts round
And, when the lamp goes, without sound
At a swifter bound
Than the swiftest hound
Arrives, and all else is drowned;

And star and I and wind and deer,
Are in the dark together, – near,
Yet far, – and fear
Drums on my ear
In that sage company drear.

How weak and little is the light,
All the universe of sight,
Love and delight,
Before the might,
If you love it not, of night.

Edward Thomas (1878–1917)

Night

There's a dark, dark wood
inside my head
where the night owl cries;
where clambering roots
catch at my feet
where fox and bat
and badger meet
and night has eyes.

There's a dark, dark wood
inside my head
of oak and ash and pine;
where the clammy grasp
of a beaded web
can raise the hairs
on a wanderer's head
as he stares alone
from his mossy bed
and feels
the chill of his spine.

There's a dark, dark wood
inside my head,
where the spider weaves;
where the rook rests
and the pale owl nests,
where moonlit bracken
spikes the air
and the moss is covered,
layer upon layer,
by a thousand fallen leaves.

Judith Nicholls

Moon

A white face
in the night.
A ten
pence piece
in the dark
of your pocket
shining
secretly bright.

A cold light
blue-circled
with winter's
frostbite.
A sliver
a shiver of ice.

A melon slice slung
in a sky spiced
with stars.
An ivory horn
still there
with the dawn.

And a great
golden plate
risen with dusk.
Coming to rest
low over fields
heavy
with harvest.

Ann Bonner

from A Booke of Merrie Riddles, 1631

> In the last minute of my age
> I doe waxe young againe.
> And have so still continued,
> since world did first begin.

> *Anon.*

from The Merchant of Venice

How sweet the moonlight sleeps upon this bank!
Here will we sit, and let the sounds of music
Creep in our ears: soft stillness and the night
Become the touches of sweet harmony.
Sit, Jessica. Look how the floor of heaven
Is thick inlaid with patines of bright gold:
There's not the smallest orb which thou behold'st
But in his motion like an angel sings,
Still quiring to the young-eyed cherubins;
Such harmony is in immortal souls;
But whilst this muddy vesture of decay
Doth grossly close it in, we cannot hear it.

William Shakespeare (1564–1616)

from What is the Truth?

To see the twilight white Owl wavering over the dew-mist
Startles my heart, a mouse in its house, remembering a dim
    past

When we were only the weight of shrews, maybe, and
    everything ate us
In a steaming, echoing jungle of night-flying alligators,

And the dawn-chorus shook the swamps, a booming
    orchestra
Where Brontosaurs were merely the flutes, and land-whales
    beat on the drum of the ear –

It has all sunk into the fern-fringed forest pool of the Owl's
    eye,
But it reaches over the farm like a claw in the Owl's catspaw
    cry.

The Owl sways, weighing the hushed world, his huge gaze
    dry and light
As a blown dandelion clock, or the moon-husk of the oldest
    night.

   Ted Hughes

Puck's Song
(*from* A Midsummer Night's Dream)

Now the hungry lion roars,
   And the wolf behowls the moon;
Whilst the heavy ploughman snores,
   All with weary task foredone.
Now the wasted brands do glow,
   Whilst the screech-owl, screeching loud,
Puts the wretch that lies in woe
   In remembrance of a shroud.
Now it is the time of night,
   That the graves, all gaping wide,
Every one lets forth his sprite,
   In the church-way paths to glide;
And we fairies, that do run
   By the triple Hecate's team,
From the presence of the sun,
   Following darkness like a dream,
Now are frolic: not a mouse
Shall disturb this hallow'd house.

William Shakespeare (1564–1616)

The Mountains Stood in Haze

The Mountains stood in Haze –
The Valleys stopped below
And went or waited as they liked
The River and the Sky.

At leisure was the Sun –
His interests of Fire
A little from remark withdrawn –
The Twilight spoke the Spire,

So soft upon the Scene
The Act of evening fell
We felt how neighborly a Thing
Was the Invisible.

Emily Dickinson (1830–86)

The Song of Finis

At the edge of All the Ages
  A Knight sate on his steed,
His armour red and thin with rust,
  His soul from sorrow freed;
And he lifted up his visor
  From a face of skin and bone,
And his horse turned head and whinnied
  As the twain stood there alone.

No Bird above that steep of time
  Sang of a livelong quest;
No wind breathed,
          Rest:
'Lone for an end!' cried Knight to steed,
  Loosed an eager rein –
Charged with his challenge into Space:
  And quiet did quiet remain.

  Walter de la Mare (1873–1956)

Miracles

Why, who makes much of a miracle?
As to me I know of nothing else but miracles,
Whether I walk the streets of Manhattan,
Or dart my sight over the roofs of houses toward the sky,
Or wade with naked feet along the beach just in the edge of
    the water,
Or stand under trees in the woods,
Or talk by day with anyone I love, or sleep in the bed at
    night with anyone I love,
Or sit at table at dinner with the rest,
Or look at strangers opposite me riding in the car,
Or watch honey-bees busy around the hive of a summer
    fore-noon,
Or animals feeding in the fields,
Or birds, or the wonderfulness of insects in the air,
Or the wonderfulness of the sundown, or the stars shining
    so quiet and bright,
Or the exquisite delicate thin curve of the new moon in
    spring;
These with the rest, one and all, are to me miracles,
The whole referring, yet each distinct and in its place.

To me every hour of the light and dark is a miracle,
Every cubic inch of space is a miracle,
Every square yard of the surface of the earth is spread with
    the same,
Every foot of the interior swarms with the same.

To me the sea is a continual miracle,
The fishes that swim – the rocks – the motion of the waves –
    the ships with men in them,
What stranger miracles are there?

Walt Whitman (1819–92)

Back Home Contemplation

There is more to heaven
than meet the eye
there is more to sea
than watch the sky
there is more to earth
than dream the mind

O my eye

The heavens are blue
but the sun is murderous
the sea is calm
but the waves reap havoc
the earth is firm
but trees dance shadows
and bush eyes turn

Grace Nichols

Answers to the riddles

from A Booke of Merrie Riddles, 1631, page 76: A swan.
Riddle *from The Exeter Book*, page 76: A swan also.
from The Girl's Own Book, 1844, page 78: Yesterday.
from A Booke of Merrie Riddles, 1631, page 119: The moon.

Index of poets

Index of first lines

Acknowledgements

'First Morning' © John Agard 1990, reprinted by kind permission of John Agard, c/o Caroline Sheldon Literary Agency. From *Laughter is an Egg* (Viking).

'Birth' © John Kitching 1994, reprinted by permission of the author.

'Firstborn' © Katherine Gallagher, 1994. From *Passengers to the City*, Hale & Iremonger, 1985. Reprinted by permission of Hale & Iremonger (Australia) and the author.

'Davy by Starlight' © Raymond Wilson 1987 from *Daft Davy*, pub. Faber & Faber. Reprinted by permission of the author and of Faber & Faber Ltd. 'There was no telling' © Raymond Wilson 1994, reprinted by permission of the author.

'The Unending Sky' John Masefield, reprinted by permission of the Society of Authors as literary representative of the Estate of John Masefield.

'I stepped from Plank to Plank', 'How the old Mountains drip with Sunset', 'One need not be a Chamber – to be Haunted –', 'The Crickets sang', 'The Mountains stood in Haze' by Emily Dickinson, reprinted by permission of the publishers and the Trustees of Amherst College from *The Poems of Emily Dickinson*, edited by Thomas H. Johnson, Cambridge, Mass: The Belknap Press of Harvard University Press. Copyright © 1951, 1955, 1983 by the President and Fellows of Harvard College.

'Whispers in the Wood' © Gerard Benson 1994, reprinted by permission of the author.

[135]